Readers Theatre

Performing the text

Susan Hill

EC

ELEANOR CURTAIN
PUBLISHING

First published in Australia in 1990
Reprinted 1991, 1992, 1995
ELEANOR CURTAIN PUBLISHING
906 Malvern Road
Armadale VIC Australia 3143

National Library of Australia
Cataloguing-in-publication data

Hill, Susan (Susan Elizabeth).
  Readers theatre, performing the text

  Bibliography.
  ISBN 1 875327 01 0

  (1).Drama - Study and teaching (Primary). (2). Readers'
  theatre   Study and teaching (Primary). 1. Title.
  372/66044

Production by Sylvana Scannapiego, Island Graphics
Design by Sarn Potter
Cover design by David Constable
Illustrations by Kate Edwards
Typeset in 12/14 Baskerville & Futura
Printed and bound in Australia

Distributed in North America by:
Peguis Publishers
100-318 McDermot Avenue
Winnipeg, MB
Canada R3A 0A2

CONTENTS

Acknowledgements

This book grew out of a collaborative effort between Wendy Parsons, lecturer in Children's Literature at the South Australian College of Advanced Education at Magill, student teachers, and teachers and their children in several primary schools. We wanted to find out how Readers Theatre worked. We had observed children performing texts in groups on many occasions and wanted to find ways to extend these ideas.

I am particularly indebted to the many students who saw the potential of Readers Theatre in extending children's knowledge of texts and enjoyment of literature. The students prompted me to document the processes I had worked through with children. A group of teachers then met in my office each week over a semester and refined the ideas further. We had loads of fun, lots of riotous laughter and much finger clicking and clapping to raps and chants. There is something quite infectious and addictive about Readers Theatre.

Students Kim Turner, James Andrews, Mary Shannon, Dianne Barrett, Julie Karutz and Mary Sofis volunteered their time to explore Readers Theatre. Teachers Jane O'Loughlin of Mercedes College and Chris Hastwell of Trinity Gardens School further refined the classroom ideas.

The children of Trinity Gardens and Marryatville Primary Schools appear in the photographs, expertly taken by Ray Stradwick. Thank you all.

Grateful acknowledgement is also made for permission to reprint copyright material: pages 32–4, 'The King's Breakfast', in A.A. Milne, *When We Were Very Young*, Methuen, London, 1924. Acknowledgement is also made of the use of traditional rhymes 'The Houchi Kouchi Dance' (page 23), included in P. Evans, *Jump Rope Rhymes*, and 'Dr Knickerbocker' (page 25), included in W. Lowenstein, I. Turner & J. Factor, *Cinderella Dressed in Yella*.

Every effort has been made to trace and acknowledge copyright. However in some cases we may have been unsuccessful. The publisher apologises for any accidental infringement and welcomes information that would redress the situation.

1

What Is Readers Theatre?

Readers Theatre is a way to make books come alive. It can be as simple as the shared reading of a picture book. At other times, when a special book is adapted into a play script, Readers Theatre can be worked up and polished into a grand performance.

Readers Theatre does not involve careful memorisation of lines. Each time Readers Theatre is performed those involved read from the text of a book or from a script. The effects that make the reading into theatre are created by combinations of voices as the group and individual readers read aloud. As there is very little action those in the audience listen to the words read and use their imagination to conjure up the images from the words.

Even a simple poem (see 'Three Little Pigs', page 24), read aloud with lots of expression by individual and group readers, creates Readers Theatre in no time at all.

Readers Theatre is a lot of fun. It can be performed by a small group or by the whole class. It is possible to give several copies of one story, poem or a book to several different groups in one class. For example, using several copies of *Hattie and the Fox* by Mem Fox, or *Arthur* by Amanda Graham and Donna Gynell works well. Each group of children can invent alternative ways to read and perform the text. One group may divide the text up so that each reader reads a line. Another group could assign various characters to the readers. Another group could click fingers and read the story to a rhythm — 1, 2, 3, 4. Another group could arrange the reading so that one reader reads most of the

text but the group joins in at times to emphasise particular words. Each group will invent quite different performances and the class as a whole enjoys seeing the variations.

Some of the features of Readers Theatre are:

1. *Shared reading:* Readers read from a shared text or copies of the same text.
2. *Group participation:* All readers participate at various times.
3. *Supportive reading:* Even if children don't know all the words they have the support of the teacher and other children to help them.
4. *Demonstrations of how texts work:* The teacher uses the text to demonstrate the reading process by drawing attention to the text organisation, meanings, words and various letter combinations.

Readers Theatre is, in fact, quite similar to the shared book experience. First of all the teacher reads the text aloud while the children follow by reading silently. Then readers participate by reading out loud with the teacher once the text is familiar. The text can then be worked up into Readers Theatre with groups and individuals reading parts of the text.

Readers Theatre does not involve elaborate costumes, props, music or lighting. A hat, a scarf or a paper crown for a king can always be used to define a character. But the emphasis in Readers Theatre is always on the images the words create, the language read and the

2

combinations of different voices that lead the readers and the audience to better understand the events of the plot and a character's goals and relationships.

VALUE OF READERS THEATRE

ENGAGEMENT, ENTHUSIASM, EXPERIMENTATION

Children engage with the text as they make decisions about what stress or emphasis a particular word should have when it is read aloud. Questions like, 'Should the emphasis or pitch rise or fall at the beginning or the end of a sentence?' demand close and attentive listening to the text as it is read. It is not unusual to see readers either lose themselves in the text or become so enthusiastic about a way to arrange the reading that time flies and another lesson has to be put aside for practice and rehearsal. In Readers Theatre each reader has to watch carefully in order to come in on cue. Even if spontaneous sound effects or music are added all readers must watch the text closely and keep up with the story and the rhythm.

Enthusiasm is created as the group of readers make decisions about how to perform the play. Creating and arranging a Readers Theatre is often more rewarding than the actual performance.

Experimentation occurs when children read the text in a range of ways to work out the best version. Often a picture book or short story has to be changed to make it work as Readers Theatre. For example, if a text has a lot of 'he saids' and 'she saids', they can be left out or given to a narrator who reads only these lines. Experimentation helps find out which way works best.

KNOWLEDGE OF LANGUAGE

Reading from a shared text or creating Readers Theatre scripts increases children's knowledge of language structure (vocabulary, syntax and meaning); language use (forms and functions of language); and their metalinguistic awareness (the ability to talk about language).

VOCABULARY, SYNTAX AND MEANING

Children extend their vocabularies and knowledge of syntax when they have sustained interactions with a well-written text. Just as big, shared books provide a model for the language children use in their own stories, so does Readers Theatre (with its repeated re-readings of a text) perform a similar function.

When children create their own Readers Theatre play scripts based on well-written stories we find clear evidence of borrowing of vocabulary, syntax and meaning from other stories. For example, in play scripts written by 5-and 6-year-old children, the children used vocabulary

NarratorI: Once upon a time there lived a little boy and two little girls.

Narrator2: They had a very mean and ugly Dad called Joshua

Dad: Go out and cut the wood

Hansel: Why do we have to do i You can do it.

Dad: Because I have to go to tow and get money. The only way can do this is if you go to the forest and cut the wood.

Gretel: But Daddy, you are lazy!

Cinderella: Why can't I go to town and Dad, you could look after the others?

Dad: Just do what I say and you won get into any trouble.

#Children: All right Dad, We'll do what you say.

NarratorI: So the chil woods

and syntax from the fairytales they had heard read aloud many times, for example:

Narrator:	There was a castle in the highlands and in that castle lived a king and queen.
Queen:	It's high time you found yourself a prince.
Magician:	Genie, Genie give me a wish?
Genie:	Only if you let me out of this chamber.
Jack:	They look like nice beans of worth.

LANGUAGE USES

Readers Theatre demonstrates the power of language to entertain, to imagine, to think, to reflect and to change ideas. Written language allows us the time to consider and explore those ideas that may pass us by too quickly in their spoken form.

LANGUAGE CHANGES

Children begin to see that by taking a simple story, Little Red Riding Hood, for example, texts can be changed around and it is possible to have many different versions of the same basic plot. When children modify stories, ranging from fairytales to complex novels, they see what it is to consider and reconsider an idea, to cross out and redraft and revise ideas so that the text works for their particular purpose and their audience. This introduces children to the more complex notion that ideas are flexible and open to change. They see that human beings are not just scripted to behave in certain ways — they can work to bring about change.

NARRATIVE STRUCTURE

As children re-read stories and create Readers Theatre from these stories they learn not only the syntax and vocabulary of books, but also have many opportunities to learn the traditional narrative structure.

The form of a Readers Theatre script is traditional narrative but one layer has been removed. There is little description and the story is told largely through dialogue. Teachers can demonstrate how indirect speech can be transformed to direct speech, for example:

Indirect speech:	The pig keeper was feeling really tired and hungry.
Direct speech:	
Pig keeper:	'I feel really tired and hungry.'

Even more dramatic dialogue can be created:

Pig keeper:	'I feel really tired and hungry. In fact I'm starving. I could eat a horse if I had some tomato sauce.'

Once the teacher has demonstrated how to change indirect speech to direct speech children are quick to invent dialogue.

LANGUAGE AND STATUS

Children quickly come to see that language changes according to status. A princess uses particular words and stresses words in a sentence in a different way from a villain (unless the princess is the villain). A king, of course, uses arrogant language, which is different from the language of a humble goose keeper.

POINT OF VIEW

When children read the dialogue of various characters they learn about point of view. For example, when planning and performing a Readers Theatre of *Charlotte's Web*, a reader could one day read with the voice of Charlotte and next day could be Templeton.

The ability to think in character has immense potential, for in effect, it allows children to apprehend another's thoughts or perceptions and make these their own. This is a conscious step to assimilate and make use of someone else's knowledge. With the conscious control over one's own and other people's knowledge comes the possibility of genuine advances, not only in personal but in social knowledge (Kress 1982).

METALINGUISTIC AWARENESS

The ability to talk about language, to describe what makes some stories effective and others less so can be developed in Readers Theatre.

EVALUATION OF EFFECTIVE LANGUAGE

When children take a picture book to make a Readers Theatre they quickly discriminate between effective and trite or contrived language. Maybe it's the rhythm of the words or the choice of rhyming words? Maybe it's the length of the sentences? Maybe the idea or focus of the story is dull or obvious? Whatever it is that makes a narrative work well becomes apparent when children read the text aloud and arrange the words for Readers Theatre.

Sometimes children rediscover an old favourite and find it works well. *Where the Wild Things Are* by Maurice Sendak, for example, is always successful when read aloud by a combination of group and individual voices. Exploring this text as it is read aloud helps children understand why this book is a treasure.

When working the story up for performance we learn and use language to describe the ideas, the organisation, the choice of language and the mechanics like syntax and punctuation in a piece of writing.

Children come to appreciate aesthetic devices like the cyclical quest pattern of the plot which is linked closely to the illustrations in *Where the Wild Things Are*. Aesthetic devices are recognised when readers experience the need for a pause in the story for the audience to catch on to what is happening in the plot. Children become conscious of

Rapunzel.   by Year R-1.

Rapunzel
(Jessica)
Prince
Witch
Victoria
Kate
Narrator 1
Narrator 2.

Narrator 1: Once upon a time there were three sisters.

Narrator 2: Their names were Victoria, Kate and Jessica.

Jessica: Let's go for a walk?

Victoria & Kate: No!

Jessica: Yes we might be able to find a nice picnic place.

Narrator 1: So they found the witch's garden and had a picnic there.

Witch: Don't have a picnic in my garden. Come with me and I'll find you a better place.

Narrator 2: They didn't know the witch was leading them to a trap.

Witch: Here's a good place for a picnic.

Victoria: There's a hedge around this garden.

Jessica: Let's get out of here quickly.

Kate: Look for a gap in the hedge.

Narrator 1: They looked and looked but all the gaps had magically closed.

Victoria: Look there's a strange thing in the sky.

Witch: Hee, hee, hee. Its me in the sky

Jessica: Look there's a path.

Kate: Let's go

Narrator 2: They walked along a path and up the stairs into a tower.

Witch: I'm outside. Rapunzel, Rapunzel let down your golden hair.

Jessica: Who is Rapunzel?

Witch: I changed your name to Rapunzel. You are RAPUNZEL!

Narrator 1: Then the witch climbs up Rapunzel's hair. But the witch didn't know that a prince was listening.

Prince: I'll wait until the witch comes down then I'll climb up. I'll save Rapunzel.

(Music)

Narrator 1: So the prince climbs up and saves Rapunzel and her sisters.

Narrator 2: He used a ladder. They went through the palace draw bridge together.

Narrator 1: They found treasure in another tower.

and learn to describe the pace and sequence of ideas and the amount of well-chosen information the reader actually needs to understand the characters and their motives.

INTERTEXT IN STORIES

Children discover the intertext between stories when similar characters and plots re-occur in fairytales, picture books and novels. These discoveries mostly come when children write their own fairytale scripts. Discussion with the teacher helps make the similarities between books explicit.

CO-OPERATIVE LEARNING AND TESTING IDEAS TOGETHER

Children creating Readers Theatre scripts work co-operatively with shared goals and goal interdependence.* All readers are needed for a performance and must support each other to succeed as a group.

This co-operative joint construction of a text not only means that children have to work co-operatively but they also have to articulate their views and substantiate their reasons for particular decisions in the group. This co-operative process has both social and intellectual benefits. Children test out ideas by saying, for example:

'What's a good way to say this?'

'Why did you do it that way?'

'What word would sound better here?'

'Let's all do it again and gradually get louder as the tension increases.'

Readers Theatre not only stimulates the mind but is also a demonstration in itself of how groups can learn communication and work together co-operatively.

* See Susan Hill & Tim Hill, *The Collaborative Classroom: A Guide to Co-operative Learning*, Eleanor Curtain Publishing, Melbourne, 1990 for details on co-operative learning.

2

GETTING STARTED

The following steps work well when introducing Readers Theatre to children:

1. **Find texts to read aloud**
   The teacher becomes familiar with poems or picture books that can be read aloud as Readers Theatre. The features of effective poems or picture books for Readers Theatre are the quality of the language, use of repetition or a cumulative structure, lots of dialogue and a strong, fast-moving plot.

2. **Introduce the text to the group**
   Start with a repetitive text like the big book *Hattie and the Fox* by Mem Fox or use warm-ups written on charts (see pages 20-9).

3. **Teacher reads aloud**
   The teacher reads the book or warm-up through so everyone is familiar with any difficult words. The children can read silently for better comprehension of the story.

4. **Read with expression**
   Choose readers and have a practice session where the readers or groups of readers read aloud. Talk about the importance of the pace of reading, tempo, volume and pitch of the reading. Children will need to watch carefully for their turn to read. Discussion about how the text can be modified so that it 'sounds better' can take place here.

5. **Rehearse**
   Rehearse and practise Readers Theatre using the same big book or warm-up poem. If there are several copies of a book like *Hattie*

and the Fox, a number of groups of children can take a copy and work up a performance for the others in the class.

6. **Conferencing and assisting**

The teacher holds a conference with each group, giving assistance as requested.

7. **Performance**

In future sessions different books can be developed into Readers Theatre. Children can then present their performance to the class.

When scripts for Readers Theatre are created the same procedure takes place. The teacher becomes familiar with the format for scripts. A script is given to the class, either on a large chart or as a photocopy. The class may read the script silently while the teacher reads. A performance of the script can then take place. In a future session, the teacher can jointly construct a Readers Theatre script with the children. Children quickly learn the script format and become keen to write their own scripts.

CREATING SCRIPTS

- The teacher becomes familiar with the format of scripts: the characters' names are on the left-hand side; narrators describe events not told in dialogue; characters speak in direct speech; characters read short pieces of dialogue; sound effects and group and individual voice are used to create dramatic effects.
- The script format is demonstrated to the class by reading scripts on charts or photocopied sheets.
- The beginning of a Readers Theatre script is jointly constructed.
- Children complete the script in groups. Usually groups of two or three work best when creating a script.
- The Readers Theatre script is performed, using group and individual voices, for the rest of the class.

When jointly constructing a script from a story it is best to start with a well-known story such as Little Red Riding Hood. The teacher asks questions like:

'How do we start?'

'What will the narrator need to say?'

The children answer and the script, made up of children's comments, is recorded on the blackboard or on an overhead projector sheet. Often the script becomes a twisted version of the story or several stories merge into each other. The scripts are never dull!

Once the children have the idea of the narrator's role — to introduce

FEATURES OF READERS THEATRE SCRIPTS

- Characters' names on the left.

- Narrators describe events not told in dialogue.

- Characters use direct speech.

- Keep the dialogue short (one or two sentences).

- Use sound effects, especially to mark time or for transitions between events.

- Use combinations of group voice and individual voice.

- Choose a fast-moving plot.

events and to explain the transitions between events — and they under-stand the structure of dialogue used in scripts (no 'he saids' and 'she saids'), they can work in pairs or threes to complete the script they began as a whole class.

BEGINNING READERS

When introducing Readers Theatre to beginning readers use stories or rhymes they already know. The main goal is to build reading confidence and enjoyment.

NURSERY RHYMES
Begin with well-known rhymes such as nursery rhymes and jingles like 'Humpty Dumpty', 'Insey Winsey Spider' or 'Five little ducks went out one day'. Even if the children can't read all the words they remember the rhymes and begin to associate the words they know with the written symbols.

ACTION RHYMES
Use action rhymes like 'Dr Knickerbocker' or 'The Houchi Kouchi Dance'. The actions in these rhymes enhance the rhythm and make it easy for all to join in.

HUMOUR
Choose poems or rhymes that will be of interest to young children. Most children enjoy humorous poems about everyday events or animals.

RHYME
Poems or stories with nonsense words build on children's appreciation and understanding of how language works to make meaning. For example a book like Dr. Seuss's *Red Fish, Blue Fish, Green Fish, New Fish* works well because it turns meaning on its head. Young children have recently discovered that language must make sense, but Dr Seuss twists this around to make nonsense, much to children's delight.

REFRAINS
Select stories or rhymes that have refrains. The refrains are predictable and are easy for emergent readers to memorise. This will ensure rapid participation by all group members.

CHILDREN'S CHOICE
Ask children what their favourites are as these will be the rhymes and stories they want to hear over and over. Such favourites often have a strong story line, repetition, humour, nonsense and sometimes action as well. Ask children for their ideas on variations of choral arrange-ments. They can experiment with the tempo, rhythm and volume as they improvise and plan performances.

FLUENT READERS

As with the beginning readers, the best way to begin to introduce Readers Theatre is by simple chants, rhymes or raps where rhyming phrases are added to a rhythm. The warm-ups on pages 20-9 are a good introduction.

Then simple picture books can be introduced. *Hattie and the Fox* by Mem Fox or *Arthur* by Amanda Graham and Donna Gynell, for example, can be read aloud and quickly arranged into Readers Theatre. Groups of readers can select a range of picture books to try out (see pages 39-44 and 80-1 for suggestions). The groups can perform their selections for the whole class or for school assemblies.

Fluent readers quickly move on to creating their own scripts and modifying novels. See 'Adapting Novels' (Chapter 6), pages 53-6.

3

WARM-UPS

Reading aloud as a group and joining in with a chant or a rhyme is a great warm-up to any lesson and a good way of building up a feeling of cohesiveness in the classroom. These warm up-rhymes, chants or street raps can be read out loud and modified in many ways. They have already been read, played with and changed by children from 5 to 12 years of age. Teachers like them too!

CHANTS, RHYMES AND RAPS

You may have heard versions of these rhymes before because improvisations on chants, raps and street rhymes by different groups often happen as they are learning them. Sometimes it is the rhythm or sometimes it is the rhyme that is changed. Once children are introduced to these chants they quickly find the beat or clapping pattern and in no time have invented versions of their own.

We all love stamping and clapping to a beat and chanting once our initial shyness is set aside. We also like to change the words around and improvise, adding a clap here, a new word there, to suit how we feel on a particular day. Although these chants have been arranged with ideas for performance the suggestions should be modified to suit the group.

Raps are also a form of rhythmic chant. They are also known as street rhymes or hip hops and are related to jazz vocalisation where a lead voice sets up a rhythm and another voice or a group voice improvises or repeats the words of the lead voice. Lots of these raps can

be traced back to the polyphony heard in African music, where a lead voice and a group voice are combined in various ways to complement a rhythm. But not all these chants and raps can be traced to Africa. Many of these rhymes are heard on street corners and playgrounds in Australia, Britain and the United States.

Some of these clapping and chanting ideas come from Bessie Jones's collection of games and chants of Afro-American origin. In her book *Step It Down*, speaking about group chants and rhymes, she says: 'Enjoy yourself. This is a beautiful democratic tradition, full of joy and the juices of life. Don't be too solemn, or too organized, these are for play'.

GETTING THE RHYTHM

To get the beat try clapping **1, 2, 3, 4** to the chants. Most chants will fit this straightforward beat. Then try clicking your fingers to one or two lines, then alternate with claps. There are some suggestions about where to clap or click or do actions included on the page with the chant. As the key idea is to have fun and improvise, these suggestions could be used on an initial run-through, then the children's ideas can be sought and followed.

Standing up as you read and chant is a good idea. This allows foot stamping and weight transference. Bessie Jones does a foot stamp movement where the left foot slides forward with the weight still on the right foot, then the weight is transferred to the left foot as the right foot steps forward. Hands clap in time and at the same side as the foot sliding forward. Trying it is the only way! After several attempts and lots of laughs you'll get it and know you've got it because it feels right.

GETTING THE VOLUME AND PITCH

Try clapping, then clicking, then stamping to the chants and you'll notice the pitch and volume change. Clapping thighs produces a different sound from clapping the back of the hand. Claps can sound high and sharp when hands are stretched tight or deep and mellow when hands are cupped. Variations of hand clapping, clicking and slapping are known as hand jiving.

FAST CLAPPING

Some of the chants are clapping games where partners learn a chant then clap their own and a partner's hands. Bessie Jones introduces this pattern which can be fitted to lots of chants:

O Each player claps hands
R Players clap right hands
L Players clap left hands
X Players clap both hands together

Try this:

O   R   O   L   O   R   O   L   X
Green Sally up   Green Sally down

O   R   O   L   O   R   O   L   X
Green Sally bake   her   possum   brown

Now clap this rhyme and try to get faster:

I asked my mama for fifteen cents
To see the elephant jump the fence
He jumped so high he touched the sky
And didn't get back till the fourth of July

READING THE RAPS AND RHYMES

The best way for everyone to see the rhymes and chants is to write them out on butcher's paper. The whole class should be able to see the words. The teacher can point to each word in much the same way as big books are read.

SILENT READING AND READING ALOUD

Silent reading as the teacher reads aloud is the best preparation for performing the chants. Children, like adults, don't like to be put on the spot by being asked to read aloud when they haven't read the material through silently first of all. Round Robin reading without preparation is to be discouraged.

ASSIGNING READERS

Readers can be selected according to their ability but putting a proficient reader with someone who needs more practice also works well. Many of the chants have group voices, some have cumulative voices as readers are added. Again improvisation is up to you.

IMPROVISE, IMPROVISE...

When the children come up with ideas for performing the raps, chants or rhymes their ideas are usually more ingenious than any adults'. Just watch the complex chanting and clapping games played outside the classroom. So enjoy yourself and have fun...

QUICK WARM-UPS

'Three Bears' begins with finger clicks *, the claps are added +. Finally on the word 'Yeah' give the thumbs-up sign.

THREE BEARS

Once upon a time
In a nursery rhyme
There were three bears * * *
A momma and a poppa
And a wee bear. * * *

One day they went a walking
And a talking in the woods.
Along came a girl
With a long golden curl.

There were three bears * * *
A momma and a poppa
And a wee bear * * *

'Someone has stolen my porridge,'
   said the poppa bear.
'Someone has stolen my porridge,'
   said the momma bear.
'Hey momma three bear',
   said the little wee bear,
'Someone has eaten my share, YEAH!'

*Goldilocks w*oke up
And br*oke up the p*a*rty.

(wave hands)

'Bye bye, bye bye, bye bye,'
  said the poppa bear.

'Bye bye, bye bye, bye bye,'
  said the momma bear.

(click fingers)

'H*ey momma thr*ee bear,'
  *said the little w*ee bear.

'S*omeone has br*oken my ch*air, YEAH!'

THE HOUCHI KOUCHI DANCE

This chant ends with the Houchi Kouchi Dance where bottoms wiggle and hands are tucked under chins. Bottoms wiggle to the 4/4 beat.
Begin by finger clicking **1, 2, 3, 4.** Two clicks are made at the end of each line.

I went down town	*	*
To the alligator farm	*	*
I sat on the fence	*	*
And the fence broke down	*	*
The alligator bit me	*	*
By the seat of the pants	*	*
And made me do	*	*
The houchi kouchi dance		

(dance to four beats)

From P. Evans, *Jump Rope Rhymes*, Porpoise Bookshop, San Francisco, 1955.

THREE LITTLE PIGS

Reader 1: A jolly old pig once lived in a sty.
And three little piggies had she.
And she waddled about saying...
Group: Grumph! Grumph! Grumph!
Reader 1: While the little ones said...
Group: Wee! Wee!
Reader 1: And she wandered about saying...
Group: Grumph! Grumph! Grumph!
Reader 1: While the little ones said...
Group: Wee! Wee!

DR KNICKERBOCKER

Dr Knickerbocker, Knickerbocker, number nine
Loves to dance to the rhythm of time
Now let's get the rhythm of the hands
(clap, clap)
Now we've got the rhythm of the hands
(clap, clap)
Now let's get the rhythm of the feet
(stamp, stamp)
Now we've got the rhythm of the feet
(stamp, stamp)
Now let's get the rhythm of the eyes
(rub finger across eyebrow)
Now we've got the rhythm of the eyes
(rub finger across eyebrow)
Now let's get the rhythm of the dance
(wiggle bottom)
Now we've got the rhythm of the dance
(wiggle bottom)
Now we've got the rhythm of the number nine
One, two, three, four, five, six, seven, eight, nine
(repeat the rhyme)

From W. Lowenstein, I, Turner & J. Factor, *Cinderella Dressed in Yella*, Hamlyn Sydney, 1982

MY NAME IS JOE

Children chant the rhyme and join in with the actions.

Hi
My name is Joe
and I work in a button factory,
I have a wife and no kids,
One day my boss says to me,
'Are you busy, Joe?'
I say 'No'.
'Then push this button with your RIGHT HAND'.
(continue pushing with your right hand as you chant.)
So I did.

Hi
My name is Joe
and I work in a button factory,
I have a wife and one kid,
One day my boss says to me,
'Are you busy, Joe?'
I say 'No'.
'Then push this button with your LEFT HAND'.
(continue pushing with both left and right hands.)
So I did.

Hi
My name is Joe
and I work in a button factory,
I have a wife and two kids,
One day my boss says to me,
'Are you busy, Joe?'
I say 'No'.
'Then push this button with your RIGHT LEG'.
(continue pushing with both hands and your right leg.)
So I did.

Hi
My name is Joe
and I work in a button factory,

I have a wife and three kids,
One day my boss says to me,
'Are you busy, Joe?'
I say 'No'.
'Then push this button with your LEFT LEG'.
(continue pushing with both left and right hands and both left and right legs.)

So I did.
Hi
My name is Joe
and I work in a button factory,
I have a wife and four kids,
One day my boss says to me,
'Are you busy, Joe?'
I say 'No.'
'Then push this button with your HEAD.'
(continue pushing with your hands, legs, and head.)
So I did.

Hi
My name is Joe
and I work in a button factory,
I have a wife and five kids,
One day my boss says to me,
'Are you busy, Joe?'
I say 'No.'
'Then push this button with your TONGUE.'
(continue pushing with your hands, legs, head and tongue.)
So I did.

Hi
My name is Joe
and I work in a button factory,
I have a wife and six kids,
One day my boss says to me,
'Are you busy, Joe?'

I say 'YES!'

OO--OO--AH--AH!

The class is divided in two. The children form one large circle with one group while the others sit in the middle of the circle. The inner circle make dreadful, spooky faces as they say Oo-oo-ah-ah.

A woman in a churchyard sat,
Oo-oo-ah-ah!
Very short and very fat,
Oo-oo-ah-ah!

She saw three corpses carried in,
Oo-oo-ah-ah!
Very tall and very thin,
Oo-oo-ah-ah!

Woman to the corpses said,
Oo-oo-ah-ah!
Shall I be like you when I am dead?
Oo-oo-ah-ah!

Corpses to the woman said,
Oo-oo-ah-ah!
Yes, you'll be like us when you are dead,
Oo-oo-ah-ah!
Woman to the corpses said —
(Silence)

Anon.

GOING ON A LION HUNT

The leader reads the words and everyone else does the actions.

Chorus: Goin' on a lion hunt,
I ain't scared.
I've got hat on my head,
And strong boots too.

1:          Comin' to some grass,
Gotta get through.
(Swish, swish actions with hands)

Chorus:
2:          Comin' to a bridge,
Gotta go across.
(Clapping action)

Chorus:
3:          Comin' to a swamp,
Gotta' go through.
(Sucking mud actions and sounds)

Chorus:
4.   Comin' to a cave,
Gotta go inside.

        . . . something warm,
        . . . something fuzzy,
        . . . it's got claws,
        . . . it's got teeth,

Now, go backwards, out of the cave, back through the swamp, across the bridge, across some grass and back home.
. . . Phew!

MORE RHYMES TO TRY

NOT RAGGED AND TOUGH!

Reader 1: At a family party held by Mr Cuff
Someone said, 'Who's been so rough
To break the vase owned by Mrs Cuff?
Was it her children, Ragged and Tough?'

Reader 2: Not Ragged and Tough,

Reader 3: But Huckem-a-Buff,
First cousin to Ragged and Tough.

Reader 2: Not Ragged and Tough,

Reader 3: Nor Huckem-a-Buff,
First cousin to Ragged and Tough.

Reader 4: But Miss Grizzle,
Ancient aunt to Huckem-a-Buff,
First cousin to Ragged and Tough.

Reader 2: Not Ragged and Tough,

Reader 3: Nor Huckem-a-Buff,
First cousin to Ragged and Tough.

Reader 4: Nor Miss Grizzle,
Ancient aunt to Huckem-a-Buff
First cousin to Ragged and Tough.

Reader 5: But Goody Gherkin,
Grandmama to Miss Grizzle,
Ancient aunt to Huckem-a-Buff,
First cousin to Ragged and Tough.

Reader 2: Not Ragged and Tough,

Reader 3: Nor Huckem-a-buff,
First cousin to Ragged and Tough.

Reader 4: Nor Miss Grizzle,
Ancient aunt to Huckem-a-Buff,
First cousin to Ragged and Tough.

Reader 5: Nor Goody Gherkin,
Grandmama to Miss Grizzle,
Ancient aunt to Huckem-a-Buff,
First cousin to Ragged and Tough.

Reader 6: But Little Snap,
Favourite dog of Goody Gherkin,

30

Grandmama to Miss Grizzle,
Ancient aunt to Huckem-a-Buff,
First cousin to Ragged and Tough.

Reader 2: Not Ragged and Tough,

Reader 3: Nor Huckem-a-Buff,
First cousin to Ragged and Tough.

Reader 4: Nor Miss Grizzle,
Ancient aunt to Huckem-a-Buff,
First cousin to Ragged and Tough.

Reader 5: Nor Goody Gherkin,
Grandmama to Miss Grizzle,
Ancient aunt to Huckem-a-Buff,
First cousin to Ragged and Tough.

Reader 6: Nor Little Snap,
Favourite dog of Goody Gherkin,
Grandmama to Miss Grizzle,
Ancient aunt to Huckem-a-Buff,
First cousin to Ragged and Tough.

Reader 1: But the feather,
Which tickled the tail of Little Snap,
Favourite dog of Goody Gherkin,
Grandmama to Miss Grizzle,
Ancient aunt to Huckem-a-Buff,
First cousin to Ragged and Tough.

All: But who had the feather?

Reader 6: Not me

All: Barked Little Snap.

Reader 5: Not me

All: Whispered Goody Gherkin.

Reader 4: Not me

All: Snapped Miss Grizzle.

Reader 3: Not me

All: Huffed Huckem-a-Buff.

Reader 2: Not us

All: Cried Ragged and Tough.

Kim Turner

31

THE KING'S BREAKFAST

Characters
Reader 1: Narrator
Reader 2: Queen
Reader 3: Narrator
Reader 4: Dairymaid
Reader 5: Alderney
Reader 6: King

Reader 1: The King asked
The Queen, and
The Queen asked
The Dairymaid:

Reader 2: 'Could we have some butter for
The Royal slice of bread?'

Reader 3: The Queen asked
The Dairymaid,
The Dairymaid
Said,

Reader 4: 'Certainly,
I'll go and tell
The cow
Now
Before she goes to bed.'

Reader 1: The Dairymaid
She curtsied,
And went and told
The Alderney:

Reader 4: 'Don't forget the butter for
The Royal slice of bread.'

Reader 3: The Alderney
Said sleepily:

Reader 5: 'You'd better tell
His Majesty
That many people nowadays
Like marmalade
Instead.'

Reader 1: The Dairymaid
Said,

Reader 4: 'Fancy!'

Reader 1: And went to
Her Majesty.

She curtsied to the Queen, and
She turned a little red:

Reader 4: 'Excuse me,
Your Majesty,
For taking of
The liberty,
But marmalade is tasty, if
It's very
Thickly
Spread.'

Reader 3: The Queen said

Reader 2: 'Oh!'

Reader 3: And went to
His Majesty:

Reader 2: 'Talking of the butter for
The Royal slice of bread,
Many people
Think that
Marmalade
Is nicer.
Would you like to try a little
Marmalade
Instead?'

Reader 1: The King said,

Reader 6: 'Bother!'

Reader 1: And then he said,

Reader 6: 'Oh, deary me!'

Reader 1: The King sobbed

Reader 6: 'Oh, deary me!'

Reader 1: And went back to bed.

Reader 6: 'Nobody,'

Reader 1: He whimpered,

Reader 6: 'Could call me
A fussy man;
I *only* want
A little bit
Of butter for
My bread!'

Reader 3: The Queen said,

Reader 2: 'There, there!'

Reader 3: And went to
The Dairymaid.

The Dairymaid
Said,

Reader 4: 'There, there!

Reader 1: And went to the shed.

Reader 3: The cow said,

Reader 5: 'There, there!
I didn't really
Mean it;
Here's milk for his porringer
And butter for his bread.'

Reader 3: The Queen took
The butter
And brought it to
His Majesty;

Reader 1: The King said

Reader 6: 'Butter, eh?'

Reader 3: And bounced out of bed.

Reader 6: 'Nobody,'

Reader 1: He said,
As he kissed her
Tenderly,

Reader 6: 'Nobody,'

Reader 3: He said,
As he slid down
The banisters,

Reader 6: 'Nobody,
My darling,
Could call me
A fussy man —
BUT

All: *'I do like a little bit of butter for my bread!'*

From A.A. Milne, *When We Were Very Young*, Methuen, London 1924. Arranged by Susan Hill.

4

USING PICTURE
BOOKS

◆

Most picture books need little adaption for Readers Theatre. Choose picture books where the language flows, and there is a definite rhythm or a repetitive rhyme or refrain. Good writing calls out to be read aloud to children: it is fresh and not trite, it creates a plausible world and it has wonder, excitement and action. It also appeals to the imagination and inspires an appreciation of the beauty of language.

Children enjoy books that show a new insight into familiar events, like losing your temper in *Angry Arthur*. They like characters doing mysterious or ridiculous things or even unfamiliar characters doing everyday things, for example pigs building houses or babies who are really tough, as in *Avocado Baby* by John Burningam.

The best way to select books that do not need adaption for Readers Theatre is by trial and error. Read picture books out loud to yourself, read them to a blank wall or best of all read part of them to the children, asking them if they think the language would work as a Readers Theatre performance. Listen carefully to the language. Books like *Drummer Hoff* work well as Readers Theatre but many other picture books may not.

Some criteria for selecting books for Readers Theatre are:
- refrains like:
  Hundreds of cats
  Thousands of cats
  Millions and billions and trillions of cats
  from *Millions of Cats* by Wanda Gag

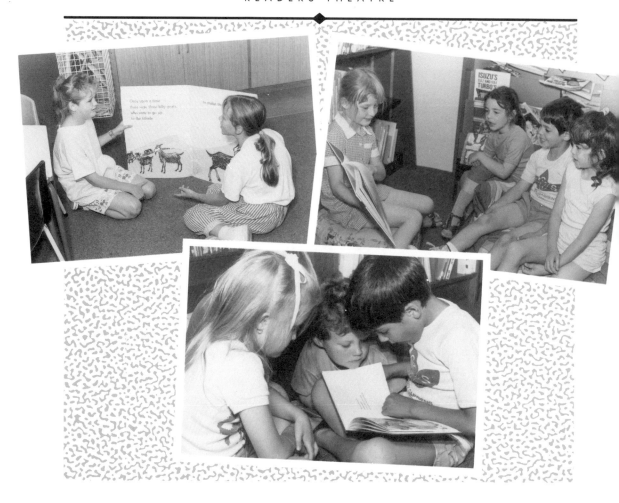

- rhyme at the end of a line like:
    Here's a little baby
    One two three
    Sits in his pushchair,
    What does he see?
    from *Peepo!* by Janet & Allan Ahlberg
- repetitive structure, e.g.:
    Is she tall?
    Guess,
    Yes
    Is she thin?
    Guess,
    Yes
    from *Guess What!* by Mem Fox
- internal rhyme, e.g.:
    Corporal Barrage brought the carriage.
    Drummer Hoff shot it off
    from *Drummer Hoff* by Barbara & Ed Emberley

- cumulative repetition like:
  Here is the maiden all forlorn
  Who milked the cow with the crumpled horn.
- repetitive structure with variations like:
  'Good grief,' said the goose.
  'Well, well,' said the pig.
  'Who cares!' said the sheep.
  from *Hattie and the Fox* by Mem Fox
- strong, fast-moving plots like most folktales and fairytales
- dramatic excitement like:
  That night in Max's room a forest grew
  and grew
  and grew.
  from *Where the Wild Things Are* by Maurice Sendak
- Heaps of action, e.g.:
  He practised
  hissing
    and slithering
      and sliding
  and looking cool.
  from *Arthur* by Amanda Graham & Donna Gynell

HOW TO BEGIN

READ THE BOOK ALOUD

After selecting a book, read the whole story out loud to the class or small group. This helps those children who may not be familiar with every word. Reading the book aloud before the children are invited to read is essential for their comprehension of the story.

DECIDE HOW MUCH EACH READER WILL READ

When a book has been selected decide how much each person will read: a line, a sentence each, a phrase, dialogue read by one person and narration by another? One reader could read the bold print and another the plain print. In time children will make these decisions but in the beginning a guiding structure or set of suggestions from the teacher is needed. (See suggestions to follow.)

DRAMATIC EFFECTS

Use dramatic effects freely to enhance the production. Simple dramatic effects include:

- pauses
- sighs

- using a chorus where all join in
- using musical instruments like drums, a triangle or a xylophone
- singing a section of the story
- adding an underlying rhythm (one reader could clap a beat)
- using recorded music as you read
- each character with a different reader's voice
- different accents for each character, e.g. an Irish accent, plum in the mouth, 'Kylie Mole' accent
- varying the speed of reading
- adding sound effects
- emphasising words like sssssssnakkkkke to create onomatopoeia.

SOME SUGGESTIONS FOR BOOKS

Hairy Maclary from Donaldson's Dairy

Lynley Dodd, Era, Adelaide, 1983

Hairy Maclary is a small scruffy dog. He walks out of the gate and is followed by one dog after another. Some dogs are small like Schnitzel von Krumm. Others are huge like Muffin McLay. They come up against Scarface Claw, a cat who scares them all. The book is cumulative, with one animal added on each page.

- Choose six readers.
- One reader is a narrator who reads any narration in between the lines describing the dogs.
- Each reader is assigned a dog's name and reads the line each time that dog is mentioned.
- Each reader can use a different accent: Schnitzel von Krumm has a German accent and Muffin McLay is British.
- All readers join in on the line 'Hairy Maclary from Donaldson's Dairy'.

Hattie and the Fox

Mem Fox, Ashton Scholastic, Gosford, 1987

Hattie, a small black hen, sees something in the bushes. None of the farm animals pays any attention to Hattie. The plot moves along quickly as the fox appears and is dealt with and sent packing. The book has a repetitive structure but there are variations in the responses of the farm animals.

- Choose seven readers.
- One reader is the narrator who reads all the 'he saids' and 'she saids'.
- Choose a reader for Hattie, a goose, a cow, a horse, a pig, a sheep.
- Try to read in character, that is the cow sounds lazy and bored and has a deep voice, Hattie is quick and frantic.
- Build up the pace slowly. Towards the conclusion anxiety is high and the pace fast.

The Napping House

Audrey Wood,
Harcourt Brace Jovanovich
San Diego, 1984

This cumulative tale is like *The House That Jack Built* because new characters are added on each page. The characters are: a wakeful flea, a slumbering mouse, a snoozing cat, a dozing dog, a dreamy child and a snoring granny.

- Assign readers for each of the six characters who read the lines for their character.
- Assign Narrator 1 who reads the first three lines of the book.
- Assign Narrator 2 who reads the three lines on the second page.

Everyone joins in softly with 'On a cosy bed in a napping house where everyone is asleep.' The reading becomes louder and faster after the climax 'A wakeful flea who bites a mouse.' Additional lines without reference to a character are read by Narrator 1.

Zeralda's Ogre

Tomi Ungerer,
Harper & Row Publishers
NY, 1967

The ogre had a terrible temper and ate little children for breakfast. Zelda came to stay and changed his taste for children into gourmet dining. The gender stereotype may be discussed in this adaption of a traditional tale.

- Assign a boy reader.
- Assign a girl reader.
- Each reads one line.
- Both join in on the chorus and menu lists.

The Cat In The Hat Comes Back

Dr Suess, Random House, NY, 1958

This nonsense rhyme has been loved by children and adults for years. The book can be read in several different ways. Characters are the Cat, Person A and Person B. It is best to experiment with reading this book, trying different combinations of voices. Sound effects can also be added.

- Select two readers.
- Reader 1 reads one line.
- Reader 2 the next line.
- Both join in on the capitalised words.

Matilda Who Told Such Dreadful Lies

Hilaire Beloc, illustrated by Posy Simmonds, Alfred A Knopf, NY, 1992

This well known verse is set and illustrated in Edwardian England. We read about Matilda's downfall as she continues to tell dreadful lies. Finally the house catches on fire and while she calls 'fire' the people only answer 'little liar'.

- Choose two readers.
- Reader 1 reads one line.
- Reader 2 the next line and so on.

Mog the Forgetful Cat

Judith Kerr, Collins, London, 1970

Mog is a very forgetful cat who always gets into trouble with Mr and Mrs Thomas. They think Mog is a bother. Mr and Mrs Thomas change their minds though when Mog helps catch a burglar. The book is a combination of narrative and dialogue. There is some repetitive structure.

- Choose five voices.
- Voice 1 reads half the narration.
- Voice 2 reads the other half.
- Voice 3 reads Mog's lines.
- Voice 4 reads Debbie's lines.
- Voice 5 reads all the other lines in quotation marks (e.g. Mr and Mrs Thomas).
- All join in on the words 'Bother that cat!'.

Seventeen Kings

Margaret Mahy, J.M. Dent, London, 1972

In North America this book is published as **Seventeen Kings and Forty-two Elephants,** Dial Books, New York, 1987

When seventeen kings decide to march through the jungle, everyone hears about it. Elephants decide to carry them, hippos dance to their music and cranes, peacocks and pelicans sing along with them. After a day of dancing and singing in the jungle the kings disappear into the rain. The book is a poem in which every second line rhymes.

- Choose two voices.
- Each voice reads one line.
- Vary the speed and volume in the different places the kings visit.

Drummer Hoff

Adapted by Barbara Emberley,
illustrated by Ed Emberley,
The Bodley Head, Toronto, 1967

A cumulative verse with steady build up of characters including
Drummer Hoff, Private Parriage, Corporal Farrell, Sergeant Chowder,
Captain Bammer, Major Scott and General Border. The verse is
similar to the traditional rhyme 'There was an old lady who swallowed
a fly'.

- Assign seven readers.
- Assign one reader as Drummer Hoff.
- Each reader reads two lines for their character.
- All join in on 'FIRE, KA BAH BLOOOM!'

Angry Arthur

Hiawyn Oram & Satoshi
Kitamura, Hutchinson,
Melbourne, 1982

This book tells the story of Arthur who has a terrible temper. Arthur's
anger becomes more and more ferocious until there is a 'universequake'
and the whole world splits up into little pieces. There are several repetitive lines such as 'That's enough' and 'But it wasn't'.

- Choose six readers.
- Reader 1 is the narrator.
- Reader 2 is Arthur and reads Arthur's dialogue.
- Reader 3 is Mother.
- Reader 4 is Father.
- Reader 5 is Grandfather.
- Reader 6 is Grandmother.
- All readers join in on 'But it wasn't'.
- All readers join in on the final line 'Can you?'.

The Very Quiet Cricket

Eric Carle, Philomel Books,
NY, 1990

A story about a cricket who could not make a sound even when he rubbed his legs together. This book has ten characters as well as the character of the very quiet cricket. The end papers of the book contain a recording of a cricket's song.

- Assign eleven readers.
- Assign two groups of readers, Group A and Group B.
- Each reads the first two lines which introduce their character.
- Group A reads 'The little cricket wanted to answer, so he rubbed his wings together.'
- Group B reads 'But nothing happened, not a sound.'

Madeline's Rescue

Ludwig Bemelmans,
Puffin, Harmondsworth, 1977

Madeline has plenty of fun and excitement in Paris. Every day she and her school mates go on outings in two straight lines. Madeline is the smallest but the bravest of all the children. A dog, Genevieve, saves Madeline from drowning and comes to live at the school. After a few upsets for Miss Clavel, the teacher, everything turns out alright in the end.

- Choose two readers.
- Reader 1 reads a line.
- Reader 2 reads the next and so on.

FOLLOW-UP ACTIVITIES

The more children interact with a text, the more ideas arise from modifying or extending that text into other forms. After creating a Readers Theatre children can:

- make puppet characters to perform the story
- make props to wear, like a king's crown
- devise a script version of the book
- create models
- make dioramas
- make a mask and write the words for the Readers Theatre on the mask.
- write a sequel or use the structure and create a new story
- write a new fairytale with a twist.

5

WRITING SCRIPTS

◆

When children have practised Readers Theatre with picture books there is a natural progression towards wanting to create their own play scripts. Play scripts work best when they are created co-operatively in twos and threes because it is easier to bounce ideas off each other than to work individually.

SCRIPTS FROM FAIRYTALES

SESSIONS 1 AND 2*

Read several versions of well-known fairytales or folktales such as Cinderella, Snow White, Little Red Riding Hood, The Three Little Pigs, and The Three Billy Goats Gruff.

Compare how each version of Little Red Riding Hood changes slightly. Sometimes a huntsman saves Little Red Riding Hood, sometimes it's a woodcutter. Sometimes Little Red Riding Hood is saved and sometimes she isn't.

SESSION 3

Draw children's attention to the parts of the plot that stay the same, for example: Little Red Riding Hood sets out for Grandmother's house;

---

* Sessions 1 and 2 are for any year level. For very young children these sessions could be extended over three or four separate lessons.

Little Red Riding Hood meets the wolf; the wolf races to Grandmother's house; the wolf eats Grandmother; Little Red Riding Hood is tricked by the wolf; the woodcutter saves Little Red Riding Hood.

Draw a diagram of the plot or a plot map showing all the events in the story.

It is also useful to teach the terminology that describes the narrative structure of a story:

Beginning (orientation): Characters and setting are introduced.

Problem (complication): A problem occurs.

Problem seems to be solved (minor resolution): Everything seems all right.

New problem (new complication): This problem is worse than before.

Problem is solved (resolution): The ending is usually happy.

Moral to the story (evaluative ending): 'Children should not talk to strangers.'

SESSION 4

Demonstrate the format used in scriptwriting and explain the following:

- Character's name goes on the left-hand side.

- Short dialogue is used to keep the story moving quickly.

- Narrator ties the story together or explains reasons for events.

- Narrator 1 and narrator 2 may be better if there is lots of description.

- Sound effects or music enhance a Readers Theatre.

- A chorus of several voices gives dramatic effect.

An example of a script to use as a model is *The Three Little Pigs* adapted by Andrew Edmonson and Kylie George. This script can be read through first by the teacher. Readers can then be assigned and the script read several times and performed for other classes. Examples of other Readers Theatre scripts are on pages 67–77.

THE THREE LITTLE PIGS

Characters

Narrator 1	Narrator 2
Pig 1	Pig 2
Pig 3	Man 1
Man 2	Man 3
Wolf	Chorus

Chorus: Once upon a time when pigs spoke rhyme
And monkeys chewed tobacco,
And hens took snuff to make them tough,
And ducks went quack, quack, quack O!

Narrator 1: Once there was an old sow with three little pigs.
She didn't have enough money to keep them.
Out they went to seek their fortunes.
The first pig met a little man with a bundle of straw.

Pig 1: Please give me some straw to build a house.

Man 1: Sure, but do you think it's a good idea to make a house of straw?

Chorus: Oh, no!

Narrator 1: The pig built a house and not long after along came a wolf.

48

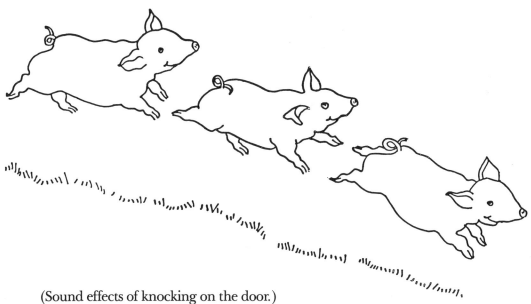

(Sound effects of knocking on the door.)

Wolf: Little pig, little pig, let me come in.

Pig 1: Not by the hair of my chinny chin chin.

Wolf: Then I'll huff and I'll puff and I'll blow your house in.

Chorus: So he huffed and he puffed and he ate up the little pig.
YUM, YUM!

Narrator 2: The second little pig met a medium-sized man with a bundle of sticks.

Pig 2: Please give me some sticks to build a house.

Man 2: Sure, but do you think it's a good idea to build a house of sticks?

Chorus: Oh, no!

Narrator 2: The pig built a house and not long after he had finished along came the wolf.

(Sound effects of knocking on the door.)

Wolf: Little pig, little pig, let me come in.

Pig 2: Not by the hair of my chinny chin chin.

Wolf: Then I'll huff and I'll puff and I'll blow your house in.

49

Chorus: So he huffed and he puffed and he puffed and he huffed and he ate up the little pig. YUM, YUM!

Narrator 3: The third little pig met a big man with a load of bricks.

Pig 3: Please give me some bricks to build a house.

Man 3: Sure, that sounds like a sensible idea to me.

Chorus: Yeah!

Narrator 3: The pig built a house and not long after came the wolf.

(Sound effects of knocking on the door.)

Wolf: Little pig, little pig, let me come in.

Pig 3: Not by the hair of my chinny chin chin.

Wolf: Then I'll huff and I'll puff and I'll blow your house in.

Chorus: Well, he huffed and he puffed and he puffed and he huffed and he huffed and he puffed. But he could not blow the house in.

Wolf: I'm coming down the chimney.

Narrator 3: The little pig hung a pot of boiling water over the blazing fire. Just as the wolf was coming down the chimney the little pig took off the lid.

Wolf: Oh, no! Youch! Yowwie! Ahhhhhh!!!!!!

Narrator 3: He screamed and scrambled back up the chimney. Off to the woods he ran and was never seen again.

Chorus: Once upon a time when pigs spoke rhyme
And monkeys chewed tobacco,
And hens took snuff to make them tough,
And ducks went quack, quack, quack O!

SESSION 5

In this session construct a script as a whole class. This allows the teacher to reteach the form a play script takes. The children come up with the ideas for the Readers Theatre script. The teacher acts as a scribe, recording the ideas the children invent.

If time runs short the children can go into groups and complete the Readers Theatre they began as a whole class. Each script will be different and children enjoy seeing these variations performed.

SESSION 6

Children form groups and construct their own scripts. Make sure each group has a proficient recorder to get the ideas down quickly. Asking older children to record the ideas for younger children is a good idea.

SESSION 7

Rehearse, revise and edit the script ready to perform for the other class members.

FURTHER IDEAS

The plays can be recorded on big books to share with other groups. In addition, smaller versions of the plays can be typed up on A4 paper and made into small booklets to keep in the library.

Children's stories can easily be made into Readers Theatre. Lots of

children's stories include direct speech so it is an easy step to make this into a script. The children learn to cut out the 'he saids' and 'she saids' to use more dialogue. They also learn to delete lots of long descriptions. This exercise of making their own narratives into a play helps children tighten their own writing and to understand how language changes according to the function it is to play.

ADAPTING FAIRYTALES

Many fairytales need only a few word changes to make great Readers Theatre. To create adaptions of fairytales find a good fairytale anthology like *Fairy Tale Treasury* selected by Virginia Haviland and illustrated by Raymond Briggs.

1. Look at lots of the stories and select those that have repetition, cumulative refrains or repetitive rhymes.
2. Read the story through carefully.
3. If the story is too long shorten some of the repetition.
4. If the story is violent you can change this.
5. Now read the story carefully line by line and write down each line, changing it if need be as you go.
6. Read the story back to the group as you go to check on how it sounds.
7. Rehearse the Readers Theatre ready for a performance.

6

ADAPTING NOVELS

Adapting novels for Readers Theatre productions creates opportunities for very close interaction and study of a text. There are three main ways to organise Readers Theatre with novels.

1. A novel read aloud to the class

Readers Theatre can be created as a group response to a novel that has been read aloud to the class by the teacher. Several groups of children can create Readers Theatre from various parts of the book. The novel could be divided up chapter by chapter or into the main events that occur in the story. In this way the whole novel can be brought to life as each group performs a section for the rest of the class.

2. A literature group

Readers Theatre is also a most effective way to explore a novel read by a literature group. A literature group could create a Readers Theatre of the chapter they are reading and discussing. This helps bring to life the personalities and motives of various characters. If the characters' motives and the plot are very complex, Readers Theatre can clarify issues previously misunderstood or not understood in a first, superficial reading.

3. Books read by individuals

Children can work collaboratively to create Readers Theatre after reading a book individually. For example, if a small group has read the book *Hating Alison Ashley* by Robin Klein, they can record their names on a chart. As soon as a group of two or more have read the book they can get together to devise a production for the rest of the class.

This will encourage even more children to read the book and further
extend the comprehension of those who have already read it.

FINDING EXTRACTS

After reading a novel, a group of three to six children can search through the book for extracts that will make effective Readers Theatre. The following features are helpful when choosing an extract to perform:

- two or more characters interact
- lots of dialogue or indirect speech to turn into direct speech
- many events occurring in a short space of time
- the personality of character(s) is developed in the extract
- a natural beginning and a conclusion in the extract. The extract should stand alone as a cameo or self-contained story within a story.

Once an extract has been found the group can take turns reading it through at least twice to check that it has many of these features. Repeated readings are necessary to begin working out how the Readers Theatre may be developed.

1. Photocopy the extract or write it out in quick draft form.
2. Cross out all the 'he saids' and 'she saids'.
3. When there is a lot of description cross this out but leave essential story information for a narrator to read.
4. Check that the narrator has only one or two sentences to read.
5. If there is a lot of essential information for the narrator to read make two narrators, narrator 1 and narrator 2.
6. Add the characters' names at the left-hand side of the script.
7. Rewrite indirect speech such as:

'Mickey said he couldn't play anyway as he slammed the door.'

and transform this into direct speech, for example:

Mickey: I can't play anyway.

(Sound effects...door slams shut.)

8. Read the script aloud to see how it sounds. Have half the group read aloud while the other half listens to make sure the script makes sense. It is easy to leave out important information. Listening to the script allows for checking that the writers have not left out information because they have become too familiar with the events and characters in the story.
9. Check that the narrator doesn't need to give more information at various transitions between events in the plot.
10. Add sound effects for scene transitions and other dramatic effects.
11. Add repetitive or additional lines where the audience is invited

to participate, for example, in *Henny-Penny* a group voice is added for dramatic effect.

All: No way!

12. Read the script through silently. If it appears to work well rewrite or retype it neatly. It is best if the script is typed up using a large print size. Charlene Swanson (1988) suggests writing scripts on a word processor so that changes are quick and easy to make. It is surprising how many small changes are made every time the Readers Theatre is performed.

7

PERFORMING

Reading with dramatic expression is essential to make Readers Theatre come alive in the mind of the audience. Warm-up sessions before each rehearsal or performance help to relax the readers and encourage creative and dramatic reading.

WARM-UPS

For warm-ups use simple rhymes or poems like those on page 20-9. If the warm-ups are written on large charts they can be used whenever needed. Warm-ups with lots of rhythm for clapping and clicking and that need different voices to join in at various times are especially useful.

VOICE PROJECTION

To encourage loud, well-projected reading explain the importance of breathing to project the voice. Ask the students to try some of these breathing exercises:

- Roll your head from the front, to the side, to the back, to the side. Breathe in and out slowly at each head position. Say the numbers 1–4 at each position, i.e. breathe in slowly at the front, exhale, say 1; then turn to the side, breathe in and out, then say 2; and so on.
- Take a deep breath and place hands under the ribcage to feel the lungs fill with air. Exhale slowly.
- Deep breath, exhale slowly as you say your name.
- Outside or in a large room facing each other, in pairs, one person

asks a question and the other answers. Now each takes a step backwards. They continue asking a question, giving an answer, and taking a step back until the pair is up to 20 metres apart.

DRAMATIC EXPRESSION

If children are reading lines spoken by a prince, a cow or a horse they
can read in a voice to match that role. Talk about the pitch and volume
use in reading. For example in *Hattie and the Fox* write the lines spoken
by the animals on a chart then try out various high / low / loud / soft
voices and see what sounds best.

'Good grief!' said the goose.

'Well, well!' said the pig.

'Who cares?' said the sheep.

'So what?' said the horse.

'What next?' said the cow.

MAKE AN EXPRESSION WHEEL

Ask the children to list as many emotions as possible and write these on a spinning wheel. On another wheel list as many characters from fairytales and popular picture books as possible.

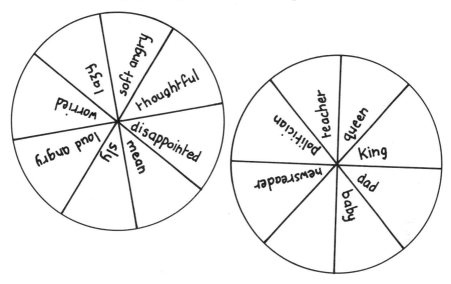

Spin both wheels and make up combinations like a soft/sad newsreader or a suspicious dad. Children invent dialogue to fit the character and the voice.

Alternatively character names and voices can be placed on cards in a hat:

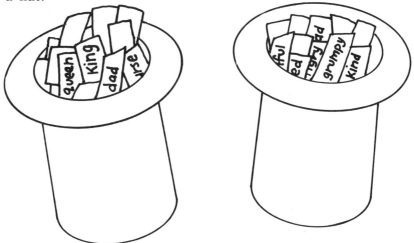

Practise using voices that express feelings. The children could choose one of the faces from A–Z shown on pages 60–1, and speak in an appropriate way for that face. A sentence like 'I've got a surprise for you!' can be spoken in many different ways.

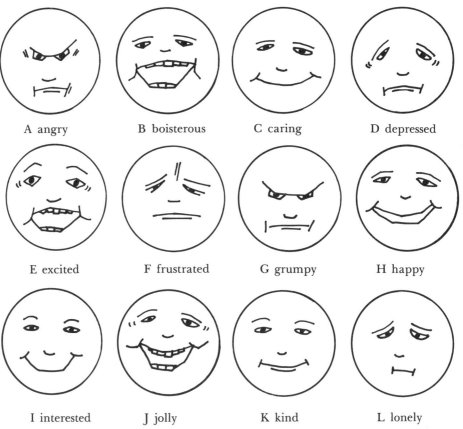

A angry   B boisterous   C caring   D depressed

E excited   F frustrated   G grumpy   H happy

I interested   J jolly   K kind   L lonely

M mischievous   N nasty   O obnoxious   P petrified

Q queer   R relaxed   S shy   T tense

U understanding   V vicious   W worried   X excited

Y yucky   Z zinging

STRESS

Stress on different words affects the meaning of the reading. Try these different stress patterns with the sentence 'My prince has come'.

My prince has come.
My *prince* has come.
My prince *has* come.
My prince has *come*.

Question and answer routines can be practised.

'Where are you going?'
'I'm going to tell the king the sky's falling.'

ARTICULATION

Children can work in pairs trying to speak these lines clearly*:

A: I live in an icehouse.
B: I live in a nice house.

A: I go to summer school.
B: I think the summer's cool.

A: I see your two eyes.
B: I see you're too wise.

A: It is five minutes to eight.
B: You have five minutes to wait.

A: Give me some ice.
B: Give me some mice.

A: His acts are fun.
B: His axe is sharp.

A: I eat Red's pies.
B: Look out for red spies.

USING SCRIPTS

In Readers Theatre scripts are usually held by each reader. For very young children it is wise to highlight the dialogue for each reader so that the right place to begin reading can be found easily.

Scripts can be written on A4 paper or on A4 paper folded over to make a small booklet. Alternatively the script may be written on large pieces of newsprint so the whole group can read from one script. Scripts can also be projected using overhead projector transparencies.

Sometimes characters in Readers Theatre productions hold a mask in front of their face. The script could be pasted onto the back of the mask so the reader merely reads from the back of the mask.

Readers Theatre scripts are used heavily, for rehearsal after rehearsal, so they can be made into books with a sturdy cover for protection.

MUSIC AND SOUND EFFECTS

Music can be used to set the scene for a Readers Theatre production. Simple sounds made on a triangle or wood blocks, and cymbals or a xylophone can be used for transitions between events or to show that time has passed. If a child is given the role of sound effects person he or she can invent sound effects to illustrate:

- a change in emotion
- time passing
- excitement rising
- knocking at the door

* From Shirley Sloyer, *Readers Theatre: Story Dramatization in the Classroom*, NCTE, 1982.

- a change of scene
- a new character entering

- links between a series of short Readers Theatre scripts

PROPS

Props can be simple. Ears for a rabbit or a wolf can be made from strips of paper. A pig's curly tail can be pinned onto jeans. A cardboard crown can be cut out for a king. The emphasis is on the words read and not on elaborate costumes.

At times readers may stand to read. Alternatively they can sit on a chair or a stool. Chairs can be used as simple props like a car or a coach for Cinderella.

THE PERFORMANCE

On the day of the performance go through the warm-up activities to relax everyone. Talk about what to do if people lose their place or jump a few lines. Make sure everyone knows where to stand and that the sound effects and props are close at hand.

If performing for a younger audience build in actions that all can do, such as clapping or squirming. The children can provide sound effects like the wind howling, or a cat meowing. Young children in the audience love to join in on refrains such as 'Yes' or 'Guess', in Mem Fox's book *Guess What!*

SAMPLE LESSON: READERS THEATRE

Subject: Drama

Objectives: Take a well-known chant or rhyme and read it aloud in a group. Use variety in pitch, volume and expression.

Materials: Copies of poems/rhymes; each group selects one to practise for performance.

Kinds of groups: Divide the class into groups of six to eight, mixing girls and boys and levels of reading ability.

Roles: Assign these roles

Director: Develops reading expression, pace of reading, helps polish reading for performance. The director's checklist that follows gives hints to improve the performance.

Director's checklist
- Can the audience see all the faces?
- Do the readers make the text come alive?
- Do the props help portray the story or do they distract the audience?
- Does the audience get the meaning of the story?
- Do you need a narrator to explain events?
- Do the sound effects help the story?
- Are the readers arranged so they are close together?
- Is the arrangement one or two boring straight lines?
- Do the readers' faces have expression?
- Should props be used?
- Should readers walk off and on stage?

Producer: Selects readers, organises rehearsals.

Checker: Checks that people come in on time, records notes on paper to help the performance if necessary.

Special effects: Decides on music or other accompaniment.

The lesson:	'Each group can take a chant from those provided. Select one that your group could practise and polish for a classroom performance. Add claps, clicks, sound effects if necessary. Assign members of the group the roles of director, producer, checker and special effects. Those people who do not have a specific role are to observe how the group encourages all to participate. You have 30 minutes to practise your piece.'
Positive inter-dependence:	All the children must co-operate to make the show a success.
Feedback and reflection:	Comment on the positive co-operative skills that were used.
End of session:	Have all the class view the different Readers Theatre performances. Discuss how the performances differed and make suggestions for improvement.

8

SCRIPTS

HENNY-PENNY

Characters: Narrator 1
Narrator 2
Henny-Penny
Cocky-Locky
Ducky-Daddles
Goosey-Poosey
Turkey-Lurkey
Foxy-Woxy

Narrator 1:   One day Henny-Penny was picking up corn when — WHACK — something hit her on the head.

Henny: Goodness gracious me! The sky's going to fall. I must go and tell the king.

Narrator 1:   So she went along and she went along till she met Cocky-Locky.

Cocky: Where are you going, Henny-Penny?

Henny: I'm going to tell the king the sky's going to fall.

Cocky: May I come with you?

Narrator 2:   So Henny-Penny and Cocky-Locky went to tell the king the sky was falling. So they went along and they went along until they met Ducky-Daddles.

Ducky: Where are you going, Henny-Penny and Cocky-Locky?

Henny & Cocky: We're going to tell the king the sky's falling.

Ducky: May I come with you?

Narrator 1:   So Henny-Penny and Cocky-Locky and Ducky-Daddles went to tell the king the sky was falling. So they went along and they went along until they met Goosey-Poosey.

69

Goosey:	Where are you going, Henny-Penny, Cocky-Locky and Ducky-Daddles?
Henny, Cocky & Ducky:	We're going to tell the king the sky's falling.
Goosey:	May I come with you?
Narrator 2:	So Henny-Penny, Cocky-Locky, Ducky-Daddles and Goosey-Poosey went to tell the king the sky was falling. So they went along and they went along until they met Turkey-Lurkey.
Turkey:	Where are you going, Henny-Penny, Cocky-Locky, Ducky-Daddles and Goosey-Poosey?
All:	We're going to tell the king the sky's falling.
Turkey:	May I come with you?
Narrator 1:	So Henny-Penny, Cocky-Locky, Ducky-Daddles, Goosey-Poosey and Turkey-Lurkey went along to tell the king the sky was falling. So they went along and they went along until they met Foxy-Woxy.
Foxy:	Where are you going, Henny-Penny, Cocky-Locky, Ducky-Daddles, Goosey-Poosey and Turkey-Lurkey?
All:	We're going to tell the king the sky's falling.
Foxy:	But this isn't the way to the king. I know a short way. Just follow me.
Narrator 2:	So they went along and they went along until they came to a dark hole. Foxy-Woxy went in first.
Foxy:	Come on in, Turkey-Lurkey.
Turkey:	Ohhh nnnoooo!

70

Narrator 1:	And Foxy-Woxy ate Turkey-Lurkey up.
Foxy:	Come on in, Goosey-Poosey.
Goosey:	Ohhh nnnooo!
Narrator 2:	And Foxy-Woxy ate Goosey-Poosey up.
Foxy:	Come on in, Ducky-Daddles.
Ducky:	Ohhh nnnooooo!
Narrator 1:	And Foxy-Woxy ate Ducky-Daddles up.
Foxy:	Come on in, Cocky-Locky.
Cocky:	Ohhh nnnooooo!
Narrator 2:	And Foxy-Woxy ate Cocky-Locky up.
Foxy:	Come on in, Henny-Penny.
Narrator 1:	But Henny-Penny didn't go.
All:	No way!
Narrator 2:	She ran home and did not tell the king the sky was falling.

Adapted by Kim Turner

RAPUNZEL

Characters:	Narrator 1
	Narrator 2
	Wicked Witch
	Rapunzel
	Puny Prince
	Mother
	Stepfather

Narrator 1: One upon a time, long, long ago in a land far away there lived a really ugly princess called Rapunzel.

Rapunzel: Oh, I'm so ugly. My face is covered in freckles, warts and pimples. Oh, woe is me.

Stepfather: Mother, we've got do do something about that daughter of yours. She's so ugly. I can't bear to look at her.

Mother: It's just a stage she's going through, dear.

Stepfather: I don't care. I don't like it. I'm going to lock her away.

Mother: That's a bit harsh, isn't it dear?

Rapunzel: Just let me try one more tube of Topex, please?

Stepfather: Never! You've had five days and it hasn't worked. I want my money back. Be off with you!

Narrator 2: And so the ugly princess was locked away in a tall, tall tower at the top of the castle.

Narrator 1: Her stepfather confiscated all chocolates, soft drink, biscuits and lollies. He called upon the terrible witch from Wart Watchers Anonymous to be her guardian.

Wicked Witch: Rapunzel, Rapunzel, let down your hair!

Rapunzel: Oh no, not again.

Wicked Witch:	Don't answer back, brat. Lift me up or you will starve.
Rapunzel:	But you're so fat and heavy!
Narrator 1:	Now for many years the witch had run a black market business for discount witches hats. Rapunzel was being exploited.
Wicked Witch:	Hurry up. I need supplies. I've got a hundred witches waiting for your discount designer hats.
Narrator 2:	Rapunzel was fed up.
Rapunzel:	I'm fed up. I wish a prince would rescue me.
Narrator 1:	Little did she know that a prince was listening.
Puny Prince:	Hark! I hear a damsel in distress. Psst! Rapunzel, Rapunzel, let down your hair.
Rapunzel:	Goodness me, my prince has come. Oh, he won't want to see me — I'm so ugly!
Puny Prince:	No, no, fair Rapunzel. I like you just the way you are. To me you are simply très magnificent.
Rapunzel:	I don't believe it: he really likes me. Pray tell, who are you and how do you know me?
Puny Prince:	Alas, I am the Puny Prince, a name given to me by my brothers. They have taunted and teased me all my life because I am so small and skinny. I have heard the wicked witch calling your name and have come to rescue you — that is, if you wish to be rescued by me.
Rapunzel:	Oh I do, I do!
Puny Prince:	Then jump, and I shall catch you.

73

Rapunzel: No offence, Puny Prince, but I don't think you could catch me.

Puny Prince: Aaah, you may be right. Well at least I tried.

Rapunzel: Oh, don't give up yet. Surely you can think of another way.

Puny Prince: I've got it!

Rapunzel: What? What is it?

Puny Prince: Cut off your hair and secure it to the window sill. Then you can climb down and run away with me. We can get married, that is, if you'll have me.

Rapunzel: Oh, of course, but let's fall in love first. And thank you for your kindness.

Narrator 1: So the princess was rescued and ran away with her prince to be married and to live happily ever after.

Narrator 2: But that didn't happen of course. They had their disagreements and disappointments from time to time. But I guess they worked those out in the end because as far as I know they're still together.

Danni Laurence and Susan Hill

THE COUNTRY MOUSE

Characters:	Narrator 1 and Man
	Narrator 2 and Woman
	Country Mouse
	Town Mouse 1
	Town Mouse 2
	Town Mouse 3
	Town Mouse 4

(Triangle sound effects)

Narrator 1:	Once upon a time in the country far away A mouse invited his cousin to stay.
Country Mouse:	Oh welcome to my humble nest. Sit right down, you need a rest.
Town Mouse 1:	Don't tell me you live in there! It very grotty and terribly bare.
Country Mouse	Come right in, it's really cosy. Come on down, you'll soon feel rosy.
All Town Mice:	UGH! HOW DULL! HOW BORING!
Narrator 2:	The country cupboard was almost bare But the little mouse found some food to share.
Country Mouse:	Here you are, you must be hungry Apples will stop you being grumpy.
Town Mouse 2:	Dried apples! I can't believe it!
Town Mouse 3:	Give me caviar! Give me gravy!
Town Mouse 4:	Give me pâté or I'll go crazy!
Country Mouse:	Barley and nut is all I can find Or what about a nice cheese rind!
Town Mouse 1:	Dear Mouse, how can you eat such stuff? I think our stay won't be short enough.
Town Mouse 2:	Life in town is heaps more fun.

75

Town Mouse 3:	You should see where we come from.
Town Mouse 4:	The food is magnificent.
Town Mouse 1:	The desserts are so succulent.
Town Mouse 2:	Not to mention the berry wine.
Town Mouse 3:	City life is just more refined.

(Triangle sound effects)

Narrator 1:	The Country Mouse's eyes lit up. On food like this he'd like to sup.
Country Mouse:	It sounds so tempting, so delightful. I'll pack my bags before nightfall.
Town Mouse 4:	A mouse doesn't live forever you know Off to the high life we'll all go.
Narrator 2:	The Country Mouse was so impressed He rushed to the door ahead of the rest.

(Sound effects: gongs ding, triangle ring)

Narrator 1:	The little mice entered a mighty mansion Their tummies rumbling in anticipation.
Country Mouse:	I've never seen food on such a scale. I feel quite dizzy and terribly pale.
Town Mouse 1:	There's turkey and ice-cream And sausages and sardines.
Town Mouse 2:	And chocolate and cherry tart I just don't know where to start.

(Sound effects: door bangs shut)

Narrator 2:	But before they could take one tiny mouthful...
Narrator 1:	In came two people on a date And loaded food upon a plate.

Narrator 2: The mice took off like lightning had struck.
One mouse hid under the cold roast duck.
Two scampered up the grandfather clock.
Others stood paralysed by the gentleman's sock.

Man: Oh dearest, this food is such a sight
Let's eat and eat all through the night.

Woman: Give me ice-cream, give me jelly
Give me more till I fill my belly.

Narrator 1: After many hours the couple had gone.
And the little mice looked quite forlorn.

Town Mouse 3: Let's go for it before I starve.
Stand aside it's my turn to carve.

Narrator 2: The little mice crept along the table
Eating all the food that they were able.

(Sound effects: MEOOWWW! MEOOWWW! Bang! Crash!)

Narrator 1: A cat came in!

Town Mouse 4: Look out! This guest could do us in!

Country Mouse: I'm not waiting, I've had enough.
This city life is way too tough.
Give me apples, give me barley.
I don't want to join your party.

(Sound effects: doors banging and a gong rings out)

Narrator 1: The moral of this story is plain to see
A dull old mouse I'd rather be.

All: WOULD YOU?

Susan Hill

77

GLOSSARY OF READERS THEATRE TERMS

Adapt: A story is changed into a play form.

Centre stage: The middle of a stage.

Cue: Lines are called out if a reader loses the place.

Dialogue: The words spoken by a character.

Direct speech: The words spoken by a character.

Entrance: Someone comes on stage.

Exit: Someone leaves the stage.

Indirect speech: The words spoken by a character are written in past tense.

Plot: The story line or events in a story.

Props: Full name is properties, i.e. the objects needed for the performance.

Rehearsal: Practice sessions.

Script: The lines read by the characters.

BIBLIOGRAPHY

Coger, Leslie & White, Melvin. *Readers Theatre Handbook: A Dramatic Approach to Literature.* Scott Foresman & Co., 1982.

Evans, P. *Jump Rope Rhymes.* Porpoise Bookshop, San Francisco, 1955.

Jones, Bessie & Hawes, Bess Lomax. *Step It Down: Games, Plays, Songs and Stories from the Afro-American Heritage.* University of Georgia Press, 1987.

Kress, Gunter. *Learning to Write.* Routledge & Kegan Paul, London, 1982.

Sloyer, Shirley. *Readers Theatre: Story Dramatization in the Classroom.* National Council of English Teachers (USA), 1982.

Swanson, Charlene C. *Reading and Writing Readers Theatre Scripts.* ARA Reading Around series, no. 1, March 1988.

Lowenstein, W., Turner, Ian, & Factor, June. *Cinderella Dressed in Yella.* Hamlyn, Sydney, 1982.

MORE PICTURE BOOKS THAT WORK WELL AS READERS THEATRE

REPETITIVE

De Regniers, Beatrice Schenk. *May I Bring a Friend?* Atheneum, New York, 1974.

Fox, Mem & Goodman, Vivienne. *Guess What!* Omnibus, Adelaide, 1988.

Martin, Bill & Carle, Eric. *Brown Bear, Brown Bear, What Did You See?* Collins Picture Lions, London, 1986.

Vaughan, Marcia. *Wombat Stew.* Ashton, Gosford, 1985.

CUMULATIVE

Bonne, Rose. *I Know an Old Lady Who Swallowed a Fly.* Collins, London, 1984.

Emberley, Barbara & Ed. *Drummer Hoff.* Bodley Head, London, 1970.

Keats, Ezra Jack. *The Fat Cat.* Scholastic, New York, 1972.

O'Toole, Mary. *The Old Woman and her Pig.* Macmillan, Melbourne, 1988.

Prelutsky, Jack. *The Terrible Tiger.* Macmillan, New York, 1973.

Wood, Audrey & Wood, Dan. *The Napping House.* Dent, London, 1987.

GENERAL

Blackwood, Mary & Argent, Kerry. *Derek the Dinosaur.* Omnibus, Adelaide, 1987.

Bodsworth, Nan. *Hello Kangaroo!* Penguin, Melbourne, 1986.

Dahl, Roald. *Revolting Rhymes.* Penguin, London, 1984.

Domanska, Janina. *The Turnip.* Macmillan, London, 1969.

Graham, Amanda & Siow, J. *Picasso the Green Tree Frog.* Era, Adelaide, 1985.

Jorgenson, Gail & Mullins, Patricia. *Crocodile Beat.* Omnibus, Adelaide, 1988.

Klein, Norma. *Girls Can Be Anything.* Dutton, New York, 1973.

Martyr, Andrew. *Beeswax the Bad.* Hamish Hamilton, London, 1988.

Nilsson, Eleanor & Argent, Kerry. *A Bush Birthday.* Omnibus, Adelaide, 1985.

O'Toole, Mary. *Kangaroo Court.* Macmillan, Melbourne, 1987.

Rothman, Joel. *I Can Be Anything You Can Be.* Scroll Press, New York, 1973.

Seuss, Dr. *And to Think I Saw It on Mulberry Street.* Collins, London, 1964.

Silverstein, Shel. *The Giving Tree*. Harper & Row, New York, 1964.

Viorst, Judith. *Alexander and the Terrible, Horrible, No Good, Very Bad Day*. Bluegum, Sydney, 1973.

Vallely, Dan & Y. Perrin. *Professor Cockatoo and his Amazing Weather Dust*. Child & Associates Publishing, Sydney, 1983.

FABLES, FOLKTALES AND FAIRYTALES

Thurber, James. *Fables for Our Time*. Harper & Row, New York, 1983.

Haviland, Virginia & Briggs, Raymond. *Fairy Tale Treasury*. Hamish Hamilton, London, 1972.

Lobel, Arnold. *Fables*. Harper & Row, New York, 1980.